10 Reasons

It's Better to
Have the Holy Spirit

10 Reasons

It's Better to Have the Holy Spirit

Andrew Wommack

Published in partnership between Andrew Wommack Ministries and Harrison House Publishers

Woodland Park, Co 80862 - Shippensburg, PA 17257

ISBN 13 TP: 978-1-6675-0040-9

ISBN 13 eBook: 978-1-6675-0041-6

For Worldwide Distribution, Printed in the USA

1 2 3 4 5 6 / 25 24 23 22

Contents

Nevertheless I tell you the truth; It is expedient for you that I go away: for if I go not away, the Comforter will not come unto you; but if I depart, I will send him unto you. And when he is come, he will reprove the world of sin, and of righteousness, and of judgment: of sin, because they believe not on me; of righteousness, because I go to my Father, and ye see me no more; of judgment, because the prince of this world is judged.

John 16:7-11

Introduction

Nevertheless I tell you the truth; It is expedient for you that I go away: for if I go not away, the Comforter will not come unto you; but if I depart, I will send him unto you.

John 16:7

If you've heard my story, you know that March 23, 1968, was a day that changed my life forever. The Lord touched my life, and I experienced a supernatural love that lasted for four and half months. What you may not know is that experience is when I received the baptism of the Holy Spirit.

Even though I was born again at eight years old, it wasn't until I received the Holy Spirit that I had the power to live a Christian life. I was living for the Lord to a degree, but I wasn't experiencing all that He had for me.

I grew up in the Baptist church and learned about the Word of God. I went on Tuesday night visitations with the church youth and shared the gospel. But I learned that I was living like a Pharisee. Even though I was doing all these things, I was doing it for myself—for the approval of other people.

> *Everything God had for me was already available when I received the Holy Spirit.*

When the Lord changed my life on March 23, 1968, it started a journey to where I am today. I began to experience a relationship with God that I didn't have before. Even though some things took me years to discover, everything God had for me was already available when I received the Holy Spirit.

Everything that the Lord has shown me and that He has done through this ministry can be traced back to that experience. I don't believe you would have ever heard of me if I hadn't received the baptism of the Holy Spirit. But because of the work of the Holy Spirit, I've seen the Lord raise up thousands of people through our Charis Bible Colleges and they are changing the world. Praise the Lord!

Jesus' Shocking Statement

Jesus' disciples were filled with sorrow when He told them He was leaving. Most believers today would feel the same way these disciples felt. What could possibly compare to having Jesus walk and talk with you?

Then Jesus shocked them by saying that having the Holy Spirit with them was better than having Him with them in His physical body. How could that be? Most Christians would prefer to have Jesus with them, as He was with the disciples.

Jesus knew His disciples would be shocked by His statement, so He prefaced it with the words "*Very truly I tell you,*" or, "*I tell you the truth.*" As hard as it may be to understand, the ministry of the Holy Spirit in the life of the believer is better than the earthly ministry of Jesus.

This is not to take anything away from His ministry on Earth. Without Jesus coming to Earth and accomplishing what He did, there could be no ministry of the Holy Spirit. The whole plan of God hinges on the redemptive work of Christ.

But once His work was done, it was actually to our advantage to have Jesus return to His Father and send the Holy Spirit to take His place

Of course, what Jesus said was absolutely true. We have to defer to the Lord's wisdom—that it's better to have the Holy Spirit with and in us than to have Jesus in His physical body. But it certainly doesn't seem like that would be true. Obviously, we don't

> *It's better to have the Holy Spirit with and in us than to have Jesus in His physical body.*

understand and value the ministry of the Holy Spirit as Jesus does.

Understanding this will hopefully bring us into agreement with Jesus that the present-day ministry of the Holy Spirit is actually better than the *limited* ministry of Jesus while He was physically present on Earth. After all, He could only be in one place at one time as a man. Even so, it would be impossible for Him to say, "*I am with you always, even unto the end of the world*" (Matt. 28:20). Yet He did say that, and the Holy Spirit confirms it to be true (see Heb. 13:5; Rom. 8:9).

10 Reasons

I teach on the Holy Spirit a lot. I talk about praying in tongues, the baptism of the Holy Spirit, and I have an entire teaching series titled *The Positive Ministry of the Holy Spirit*. Recently, the Lord spoke to me about this teaching that encompasses ten truths about how life is better having the Holy Spirit in us than it is to have Jesus in His physical body with us. That's a powerful statement, but it is exactly what Jesus told His disciples.

Most Christians think that if they saw a physical manifestation of Jesus standing right in front of them, it would be awesome. But Jesus said it's actually better to have the Holy Spirit. Most would disagree because they don't have a full understanding of who the Holy Spirit is and what He does.

I could teach on every one of these ten aspects of the Holy Spirit for at least a couple of hours, but this book highlights the most intimate qualities and characteristics of the Holy Spirit. I think you'll really be blessed to discover these things that the Lord revealed to me.

1

The Holy Spirit in Us

Nevertheless I tell you the truth; It is expedient for you that I go away: for if I go not away, the Comforter will not come unto you; but if I depart, I will send him unto you.

John 16:7

While on Earth, Jesus was limited by His physical body. He could only be in one place at a time. Therefore, He was not always present with everyone who believed on Him. But as He was ascending to heaven, He promised He would be with us *"unto the end of the world"* (Matt. 28:20). Now, Jesus is constantly with each believer. Jesus will never leave or forsake even one true Christian (see Heb. 13:5).

When someone is born again, Jesus comes and lives inside that person. Paul says in Galatians 4:6, *"God hath sent forth the Spirit of his Son into your hearts, crying, Abba, Father."* Some Christians have a hard time believing this because they can't see or feel Jesus inside them. But Paul said again in Romans 8:9, *"...if any man have not the Spirit of Christ, he is none of his."* Therefore, this is reality, whether a person believes it or not. To benefit fully from this truth, we have to believe in order to receive (see Heb. 4:2).

When someone is born again, Jesus comes and lives inside that person.

On resurrection morning, two of Jesus' disciples were walking to Emmaus, which was about seven miles from Jerusalem (see Luke 24:13-32). They had heard reports that Jesus was raised from the dead, but they were struggling to believe it. That's why they were sad.

As they walked, the resurrected Jesus joined them and explained from the Scriptures how He had to die and be resurrected on the third day. They were walking and talking with Jesus for miles, and yet they didn't even recognize Him. It wasn't until they were breaking bread with Him that they realized who He really was.

If that could happen then, it's even more so now that we can't see Him. And likewise, it is only through fellowship with the risen Lord that we realize His presence with us now. As soon as we are born again, Jesus is with us constantly. That can only happen through the Holy Spirit.

There are few things more controversial in the body of Christ than the baptism of the Holy Spirit and the accompanying gifts. Much of modern-day Christianity sees the

> *It is only through fellowship with the risen Lord that we realize His presence with us now.*

born-again experience as all there is to salvation. Unfortunately, some Christians oppose the belief that there is a separate experience of being filled with the Holy Spirit, and they especially oppose the validity of the gifts of the Holy Spirit for believers today.

Many people don't really receive the benefit from that wonderful gift because they can't see Him. They can't feel Him with natural, human feelings, so they aren't aware.

But the spiritual reality is that Jesus is now *in* us through the Holy Spirit dwelling in us!

2

Born of the Spirit

Jesus answered, Verily, verily, I say unto thee, except a man be born of water and of the Spirit, he cannot enter into the kingdom of God. That which is born of the flesh is flesh; and that which is born of the Spirit is spirit. Marvel not that I said unto thee, Ye must be born again. The wind bloweth where it listeth, and thou hearest the sound thereof, but canst not tell whence it cometh, and whither it goeth: so is every one that is born of the Spirit.

John 3:5-8

T he second reason why life is better with the Holy Spirit is that when we make Jesus our Lord and receive salvation, we are born of the Holy Spirit.

In John chapter 3, Jesus said three times that we have to be born of the Spirit.

Jesus answered, Verily, verily, I say unto thee, except a man be born of water and of the Spirit, he cannot enter into the kingdom of God.

John 3:5

That which is born of the flesh is flesh; and that which is born of the Spirit is spirit.

John 3:6

The wind blows where it listeth, and thou hearest the sound thereof, but canst not tell whence it cometh, and whither it goeth: so is every one that is born of the Spirit.

John 3:8

So, if the Holy Spirit had not come, believers could not be born again. There couldn't be a born-again experience until the Holy Spirit came.

Jesus says in John 7:38, *"He that believeth on me, as the scripture hath said, out of his belly shall flow rivers of living water."* Rivers of living water flowing out of us are produced by the Holy Spirit when people believe on Jesus. But this couldn't happen until after the resurrection.

The Holy Spirit is intimately involved in our salvation and baptizes us into the body of Christ. The apostle Paul says in 1 Corinthians 12:13, *"For by one Spirit are we all baptized into one body, whether we be Jews or Gentiles, whether we be bond or free; and have been all made to drink into one Spirit."* You couldn't be part of the body of Christ without the Holy Spirit.

This couldn't happen while Jesus was on Earth before His death and resurrection—the Holy Spirit is the One who brings our new birth to pass. The Church wouldn't exist without the ministry of the Holy Spirit.

As believers, we should recognize the importance of the Holy Spirit's role in our salvation.

> *The Holy Spirit is the One who brings our new birth to pass.*

At salvation, the Holy Spirit seals us so that when a Christian commits sin, it doesn't penetrate the seal and contaminate our born-again spirit. Our spirits have eternal redemption (see Heb. 9:12), eternal salvation (see Heb. 9:15), are sanctified (see Heb. 10:10), and perfected forever (see Heb. 10:14) because of the preserving power of the Holy Spirit. Praise the Lord!

3

Revelation Knowledge

*But the natural man receiveth not **the things of the Spirit of God**: for they are foolishness unto him: neither can he know them, because they are **spiritually discerned**.*

1 Corinthians 2:14

Without the Holy Spirit we would not be able to perceive spiritual things.

When I received the baptism of the Holy Spirit, there was an emphasis on speaking in tongues (more on that later), but the dominant thing I received from the Holy Spirit was that the Bible came alive! It was like a brand-new book to me. I could not get enough of it.

Those two men who were walking to Emmaus didn't recognize Jesus—yet later that day they said, *"Did not our heart burn within us, while he talked with us by the way, and while he opened to us the scriptures?"* (Luke 24:32).

The Scripture says people wrote as they were inspired by the Holy Spirit—the Holy Spirit wrote the Word of God, the Bible. He will enlighten it to every believer—to you.

Spiritual things can only be revealed by the Holy Spirit (see 1 Cor. 2:14). Prior to the infilling of the Holy Spirit, we are dull to the things of God.

It says in 1 Corinthians 2:14, *"the natural man receiveth not the things of the Spirit of God: for they are foolishness unto him: neither can he know them, because they are spiritually discerned."*

Spiritual things can only be revealed by the Holy Spirit.

This is why so many Christians get stuck. They're trying to figure out the Word of God with their brain. The Bible is written to your heart. You have to receive it by Holy Spirit revelation.

Jesus tells us in John 14:26:

*But the Comforter, which is the Holy Ghost, whom the Father will send in my name, he **shall teach you all things**, and **bring all things to your remembrance**, whatsoever I have said unto you.*

The Holy Spirit wrote God's Word (see 2 Pet. 1:21) and He will reveal it (see 1 Cor. 2:9-10). Our understanding has to be opened through the Holy Spirit to know God's Word (see Luke 24:45). The Holy Spirit reveals Jesus to us (see John 15:26). We can know Jesus better through the ministry of the

> *Our understanding has to be opened through the Holy Spirit to know God's Word.*

Holy Spirit than the disciples knew Him through physical things (see 2 Cor. 5:16).

The apostle Paul said he had known Jesus after the flesh once, but now he only knew Jesus after the Spirit. And Paul, through the Spirit, had a revelation of Jesus that made even the apostle Peter marvel (see 2 Pet. 3:15-16). Peter acknowledged Paul's writings were scripture, but he said they were hard to understand.

Think about that.

Peter, who spent three and a half years with Jesus, day and night, didn't understand the teachings of Jesus as well as Paul, who only met Jesus after He was back in heaven. Likewise, we can know Jesus better through the revelation of the Holy Spirit than if we were physically with Him.

I have a short teaching on this titled *Are You Satisfied with Jesus?* Jesus' physical body actually cloaked who He really was. Isaiah 53:2 says Jesus' body wasn't special and there was "*no beauty that we should desire him.*" Amazing!

Today, we don't have a physical hinderance that limits our perception and acceptance. We can see Him by the Spirit and envision Him in all of His glory. We are more blessed than His original disciples!

The Holy Spirit will teach you all things—not just some things, but *all* things. And He will lead you into all truth and bring to your remembrance what you need to know. That's powerful!

> *The Holy Spirit will teach you all things—not just some things, but all things.*

One reason people fall away from the Lord is because they don't rehearse their victories and remember what God has done for them. The Holy Spirit will teach you, lead you into truth, and bring to your remembrance all He has done for you. He will give you spiritual perception. If you haven't been baptized in the Holy Spirit, you need to be.

4

Power

*But **ye shall receive power**, after that the Holy Ghost is come upon you: and ye shall be witnesses unto me both in Jerusalem, and in all Judaea, and in Samaria, and unto the uttermost part of the earth.*

Acts 1:8

The last thing Jesus told His disciples before He ascended into heaven was, *"you shall receive power"* (Acts 1:8). The word "power" used here is from the Greek *dynamis* (doo'-nam-is)—where we get our words "dynamite" or "dynamo"—as in miraculous, miracle-working power. This is the type of power you receive when the Holy Spirit comes upon you.

You can see the difference in the disciples before and after they received the Holy Spirit. Before the Day of Pentecost, they were fearful men—they ran and they denied the Lord. But after they received the Holy Spirit, they were stronger than horseradish!

Even the Sanhedrin, when they saw the disciples' boldness, took note of them that they had been with Jesus (see Acts 4:13). And that was because of the Holy Spirit.

I'll tell you, we could use some of that boldness today with all the things going on and the spirit of antichrist at work in the world. People are just timid and shy, but the Holy Spirit will give you supernatural power.

Some Christians willingly accept a limited ministry of the Holy Spirit as their Comforter and Consoler yet deny His miraculous power. They want to enjoy the benefits without the responsibility. They believe there is no second Holy Spirit experience beyond being born again. They may be sincere in their beliefs, but they are sincerely wrong.

There are many clear examples in Scripture where a miraculous encounter with the Holy Spirit enabled believers to be empowered to live supernatural lives. Jesus taught about two separate experiences in the believer's life. For example, in John 20:28, Thomas confessed Jesus as his Lord and God. That made him "saved" according to Romans 10:9-10.

Yet, the Lord told Thomas and all the disciples to tarry in Jerusalem until they received the power of the Holy Spirit (see Acts 1:4), because they didn't have it yet. After the disciples received that power, they were changed men.

After the Day of Pentecost, when the Holy Spirit came upon Jesus' disciples, they became powerful and bold.

> *After the disciples received that power, they were changed men.*

They faced persecution and death fearlessly. What made the difference? By Jesus' own words, it was the baptism of the Holy Spirit.

It's easy to see the contrast between the disciples *before* they received the Holy Spirit and *after* they received the Holy Spirit.

Before	After
Fearful	Bold
Denied Jesus	Proclaimed Jesus
Timid and shy	Empowered
Limited by flesh	Spiritually gifted
(See Matt. 26:56; Mark 14:50)	(See Acts 4:13,31; 19:8)

Christians today need this power of the Holy Spirit to boldly proclaim Jesus as the Savior He is and to be ready to stand against evil (see Eph. 6:10-18). We have the supernatural power to defeat the spirit of antichrist. Believe it!

Power to Change

We receive miracle-working power when the Holy Spirit comes and resides within us (see Acts 1:8).

I believe that the number-one reason people resist the ministry of the Holy Spirit today is because it exposes the lack of power in their lives. And once exposed, it demands a change. In an attempt to avoid responsibility for change, they change the Scriptures instead of themselves. Of course, it's not that blatant; but there is a predisposition against the ministry of the Holy Spirit, so the Scripture is twisted to support their views.

> *We receive miracle-working power when the Holy Spirit comes and resides within us.*

It's now "politically correct" to say that alcoholics are not responsible for their actions, depression is a chemical imbalance, and homosexuality is genetic. There have even been lawsuits where overweight people sue fast-food chains for their obesity. No one wants to admit that their lives are the result of their own choices and actions. It's appealing to think that someone else is at fault for their messed-up lives. Sadly, the lack of personal responsibility in our society has crept into the attitudes of the church.

The ultimate attempt to avoid responsibility is when we place the blame on God. This goes all the way back to Adam when he said, "It's that woman *You* gave me—*she* gave it to me to eat" (Gen. 3:11, paraphrased). Adam passed the buck to the woman and then ultimately blamed God. But God's judgment held Adam responsible for his own actions.

Always remember, you receive power from the Holy Spirit that gives you the boldness to make the right decisions, accept responsibility, and overcome and declare victory in every aspect of life.

5

Remembering All

*But the Comforter, which is the Holy Ghost, whom the Father will send in my name, he shall teach you all things, and **bring all things to your remembrance**, whatsoever I have said unto you.*

John 14:26

The fifth reason that life is better with the Holy Spirit is that He teaches us—He reminds us of what Jesus has said. I've already mentioned how the Holy Spirit quickens our spiritual ability, but now we're concentrating on how He helps us remember important spiritual truths. And I tell you, this is a really powerful gift from the Holy Spirit.

When I first got turned on to the Lord, I used to take notes. Anything people said, I would write pages and pages of notes. Then I'd go back and read my notes after a year or so. And often I'd think, *That's not God—this isn't right.* Then I just decided I was going to stand on John 14:26. I chose to believe that the Holy Spirit would bring back to my remembrance what Jesus said, and I could just miss all that other stuff.

I don't think most people fully understand how important memory is. In one of my teachings, *Discovering the Keys to*

Staying Full of God, I stress the importance of memory when it comes to being thankful. It's important to remember what God has done in your life.

Psalm 103:1-2 says, *"Bless the Lord, O my soul: and all that is within me, bless his holy name. Bless the Lord, O my soul, and forget not all his benefits."* Don't forget the blessings, miracles, and things that God has done in your life. The reason it's a command to remember is because it's our tendency to forget.

Did you know memory takes effort? A lot of people don't realize this, but you need to intentionally go back and remember the goodness of God in your life.

The apostle Peter, when he knew his time to die was near, told the people, *"Wherefore I will not be negligent to put you always in remembrance of these things, though ye know them, and be established in the present truth. Yea, I think it meet, as long as I am in this tabernacle, to stir you up by putting you in remembrance"* (2 Pet. 1:12-13).

Don't forget the blessings, miracles, and things that God has done in your life.

Peter says that memory will stir you up. I have literally hundreds of examples of how memory has affected me.

March 23, 1968, is something I think about every day of my life. I was already born again, but that's the day the power of the Holy Spirit came into my life and the Lord rang my bell—and I remember it!

I've also kept a journal since 1996, writing down things that happen, and I look through it to help remember the good things God has done for me.

The Holy Spirit reminds you of the goodness of God.

Like Peter says, if you're not reminding yourself and others of what God has done, you're being negligent. You can get so caught up in what's going on in your own life that you can forget about the goodness of God. If you're not stirring yourself up, you're going to sink to the bottom.

This is one of the ministries of the Holy Spirit: to bring *"to your remembrance whatsoever"* Jesus has spoken *"unto you"* (John 14:26). One of the reasons why it is better to have the Holy Spirit with you than the physical presence of Jesus is that the Holy Spirit reminds you of the goodness of God.

When you go back and remember how good God has been to you and that He has never failed you, it will give you hope and confidence for the future.

6

Show Things to Come

Howbeit when he, the Spirit of truth, is come, he will guide you into all truth: for he shall not speak of himself; but whatsoever he shall hear, that shall he speak: and he will shew you things to come.

John 16:13

John 16:13 says that the Holy Spirit *"will shew* [tell] *you things to come."* I'll tell you, this is so important. Most Christians go through life like a blind person. They go about their daily lives not seeing what is right in front of them. It's just a matter of time until they trip over something, run into something, or get hit by something. The average Christian just goes through life without any supernatural direction.

But Jesus says in John 16:13, the Holy Spirit will tell you things to come! I can give you hundreds of examples of when the Lord has told me about something that was going to happen.

Two examples:

There was a guy who had everything going for him. He was the mayor of the city. He looked great. And he wanted to be my best friend. I admit I was flattered. But the Lord spoke to me through the Holy Spirit and told me to stay away from that guy—far away. He said the guy was a wolf in sheep's clothing. And it turned out to be so!

During the Great Recession in 2008, the Holy Spirit spoke to my wife about her father's inheritance that we had invested. He told her to pull everything out of the stock market. We did and shortly afterward the stock market plunged. When we were told to reinvest, we made 60 percent while everybody else was losing 60 percent.

Some people think that may not be true, but don't wake me up, because that's how we're living. Praise the Lord for the Holy Spirit telling me of things to come!

Holy Spirit Warnings

The Holy Spirit will tell you things to come. That's true and good. The Holy Spirit also warns you. He has told us what He wants us to do regarding Charis Bible College—about the buildings, grounds, etc. When we know it's from Him, we obey!

Most people do their own thing and then say, "God, bless this. We ask You to bless

> *Praise the Lord for the Holy Spirit telling me of things to come!*

> *When God is the Author of it, it will work.*

it." If you first find out what God wants you to do and follow His directions, you don't have to ask God to bless it. I never have to ask God to bless what I'm doing because I only do what God says and the Holy Spirit shows me. I don't have any desire or any agenda other than to do His will.

If the Holy Spirit tells and/or shows you what to do, you can count on it being to your benefit. When God guides, He will provide. When God is the Author of it, it will work. You can know that regardless of any opposition that comes against you, it will not prosper (see Isaiah 54:17).

One of the reasons so many people fail in their faith is because they honestly don't have the confidence that the Holy Spirit has directed them. They hope that He has, they pray that He has, but they don't have that confidence that He did. Because of that lack of confidence, Satan can come in and steal things. If you don't have faith and confidence in God's Holy Spirit, you will fall apart like a two-dollar suitcase when troubles come.

Knowing that the indwelling Holy Spirit shows you and leads you and tells you what's going to happen will cause you to win and not fail—that's priceless!

7

Holy Spirit Gifts

*But the manifestation of the Spirit is **given to every man to profit withal**. For to one is given by the Spirit the **word of wisdom**; to another the **word of knowledge** by the same Spirit; to another **faith** by the same Spirit; to another the gifts of **healing** by the same Spirit; to another the working of **miracles**; to another prophecy; to another **discerning of spirits**; to another **divers kinds of tongues**; to another the **interpretation of tongues**: But all these worketh that **one and the selfsame Spirit**, dividing to every man severally as he will.*

1 Corinthians 12:7-11

So, why is there so much debate over the gifts of the Holy Spirit? The sad truth is that denial of the ministry and power of the Holy Spirit is a convenient theology. Believing that miracles and gifts of the Holy Spirit don't operate today excuses powerless living. The Holy Spirit was willing to move in biblical times *and* the Holy Spirit is willing to move *today*. There is no excuse for living lives so far removed from the victory portrayed in God's Word.

The most controversial gift is praying and speaking in *"different kinds of tongues."* Speaking in tongues is not only

> *There is no excuse for living lives so far removed from the victory portrayed in God's Word.*

one of the first things that happens after being baptized in the Holy Spirit, but it's also one of the most important.

When you pray in tongues, it says in 1 Corinthians 14:14 that your spirit prays. Your spirit is the part of you that is born again, that has the mind of Christ. First Corinthians 2:16 says that *"we have the mind of Christ,"* that your mind has been renewed in knowledge of your Creator (see Col. 3:10). So, in your spirit, you have the mind of Christ. You have unlimited knowledge, and all you have to do is draw it out.

How do you draw out the godly wisdom that's in your spirit? The Bible says that when you pray in tongues, your spirit, the part of you that has that knowledge, is praying (see 1 Cor. 12:14). If you pray in tongues, 1 Corinthians 14:13 says to pray also for interpretation of tongues.

I have prayed in the spirit many times when confronted with something in the natural that I just didn't have the ability to conquer—just didn't have the self-confidence. So I go to prayer in tongues. I need the Lord, and I don't lean on my own understanding.

When I run into a problem, I pray in tongues and ask God for wisdom. I also pray for God to give me the interpretation. If I'm praying and nobody else is around, I don't need to speak it out. I just need my understanding enlightened. I could give you testimony after testimony about how this special communication with God has blessed me.

You have unlimited knowledge, and all you have to do is draw it out.

One of the most miraculous occurrences in my life was when we were waiting on a $3.2 million loan for a building project. The process was dragging out so long that they wanted us to start the whole process over. So I said, "God, there's got to be an answer. What is the answer to this situation?" I started praying in tongues and asked Him what to do and for the interpretation. It wasn't two minutes later when the Lord spoke to me a prophecy that had come to me two years before. I hadn't denied it. I just hadn't remembered it. The prophecy was that I didn't need a bank loan; my partners would finance whatever I needed. Fourteen months later we had the $3.2 million, which propelled us into a new realm of prosperity and blessing that we had never had. And all of that came from praying in tongues and praying for an interpretation.

> *We must understand that we have the mind of Christ and all of His wisdom is flowing in and through us.*

We must understand that we have the mind of Christ and all of His wisdom is flowing in and through us. Not realizing this truth is like dying of thirst while leaning against a well filled with water because you don't know how to draw it out. Speaking in tongues is drawing out the Holy Spirit and then praying that you receive the interpretation from God.

The Gift

I guess it's possible to have the baptism of the Holy Spirit and not speak in tongues, but why wouldn't you want to? If you're afraid, don't be! There's no reason to fear; you're in full control. I'm not speaking in tongues as I write this, because it's up to me to decide when I speak in tongues. It's the same for you. You control when you speak in tongues.

Maybe there's something else that is holding you back. I've seen firsthand how someone who doesn't have the proper perspective on this gift can stifle it. I did. In my case, a denomination had instilled such fear in me that I was afraid

I would get something from the devil. It wasn't until later that I learned the Lord wouldn't let that happen (see Luke 11:13).

Whether you're not sure or just having a problem receiving, my teaching titled *The New You & the Holy Spirit* will answer your questions and set you free to receive this powerful gift. My life was completely changed when I received the Holy Spirit. If it were not for that, you would never have heard of me.

And my teaching *The New You & the Holy Spirit* is the same material I give to those who receive the baptism of the Holy Spirit at our Gospel Truth Seminars. It shares very practical steps on how to receive the gift of speaking in tongues. Hundreds of people who were having trouble speaking in tongues were able to receive after reading the book or listening to this teaching. You may know people who haven't received the baptism of the Holy Spirit, and this teaching could forever change their lives. Yours as well.

8

Fruitfulness

*But the **fruit of the Spirit** is love, joy, peace, longsuffering, gentleness, goodness, faith, meekness, temperance: against such there is no law.*

Galatians 5:22-23

The eighth reason that life is better with the Holy Spirit is the fruit of the Holy Spirit. And again, I could teach on this for multiple hours, but Galatians 5:22-23 says the fruit of the Spirit is *love, joy, peace, longsuffering, gentleness, goodness, faith, meekness,* and *temperance.* Notice that the scripture says the "*fruit*"—not fruits—of the Spirit. It lists nine things, but it's just one fruit.

It's like a prism when the sunlight hits it and the full color spectrum is displayed—yet coming from one source. The fruit of the Spirit is a package deal. If you have love, you also have joy and peace and longsuffering, gentleness, goodness, faith, meekness, and temperance. We could examine each of those, but I'd like to focus on temperance. Nearly every modern translation of the Bible presents it as "self-control," but if you look up the word "temperance" in the Greek, it is specifically self-control in food and drink. The effort back in the 1800s aimed to prohibit alcohol was called the "temperance movement."

And so, temperance is self-control, specifically in food and drink. I'll tell you, gluttony is the Christian sin.

> *The fruit of the Spirit is a package deal.*

There are a lot of overweight Christians. And you know what? God loves them. I love them. I'm not against them, but I'm saying it is sin. It's listed right along with adultery, murder, stealing, and everything else sinful. We have to eat. So you can't just swear off food, but you have to have temperance, or self-control, specifically in this area.

If you are born again, you also have a supernatural peace, along with faith, love, joy, and all of the fruit of the Spirit. Now it may not be dominant in your life, because you can walk in the spirit or you can walk in the flesh, but in your spirit you do have this fruit.

The apostle Paul, in Colossians 3:15, says, *"let the peace of God rule in your hearts."* In this verse, the word "rule" comes from a Greek word that means "umpire." Just like in baseball, where an umpire calls balls and strikes, the supernatural peace provided by the Holy Spirit can help us make decisions.

One of the most important decisions I had to make came after the Lord touched my life on March 23, 1968. I was in college at the time, but after that night I lost all desire to go to school. When I told people I was planning to leave college, my family and church came out against it. I also risked losing the $350 I received from my father's Social Security benefits and I would immediately become eligible to serve in the military—which meant a first-class ticket to Vietnam.

Considering these things, I backed off my decision for a while, but I was miserable. As I prayed and studied the Word for guidance, I found Colossians 3:15.

The Lord told me to head in the direction that gave me the most peace. I had the most peace about quitting school, so I made my decision. Within 24 hours the Lord confirmed it and gave me so much joy that I have never doubted the wisdom of that decision since. That one decision, possibly more than any other, set my life on a course that has brought me to where I am today.

All you have to do is just turn away from the natural things that occupy you: opinions of people, criticism, and fear of failure. Turn away from those things and follow what the Spirit is leading you to do. There's always peace in the direction that God wants you to go.

There's always peace in the direction that God wants you to go.

I focused on just a few aspects of the fruit of the Spirit in this chapter, but we need *all* of the fruit if we're going to be successful in this life. Living the Christian life isn't just difficult; it's impossible without the power of the Holy Spirit!

9

Comforted to Comfort

*Blessed be God, even the Father of our Lord Jesus Christ, the Father of mercies, and the God of all comfort; who comforteth us in all our tribulation, **that we may be able to comfort them which are in any trouble, by the comfort wherewith we ourselves are comforted of God.***

2 Corinthians 1:3-4

The ninth reason that life is better with the Holy Spirit is the comfort He brings us. The night before His crucifixion, He told the disciples about the Comforter:

*Nevertheless I tell you the truth; It is expedient for you that I go away: for if I go not away, the **Comforter** will not come unto you; but if I depart, I will send him unto you.*

John 16:7

He called the Holy Spirit "the Comforter." From time to time all people, even Christians, need to be comforted. The trials and tribulations of life can get us down—but we can be comforted and revived knowing that Jesus' parting gift was the Comforter.

I ministered to a very good friend of mine when his wife was just about to go home to be with the Lord. He said all the family was with him as she would probably die in the next few days. I told him, "I'm really glad for her because

> *He called the Holy Spirit "the Comforter."*

she's been suffering. When she passes into heaven, she will be more alive than ever. And I'm praying that the Holy Spirit will comfort you."

> *Blessed be God, even the Father of our Lord Jesus Christ, the Father of mercies, and the God of **all comfort**; who **comforteth** us in all our tribulation, that we may be able to **comfort** them which are in any trouble, by the **comfort** wherewith we ourselves are **comforted** of God.*
> **2 Corinthians 1:3-4**

I could say that to my friend because of what Paul wrote to the Corinthians. The Comforter will comfort you in all your tribulations—so that you will know how to comfort other people. We are blessed to bless; we are comforted to comfort—individually and as the body of Christ as a whole.

> *Then had the churches rest throughout all Judaea and Galilee and Samaria, and were edified; and walking in*

> *When people are ragging on you and bad things happen, never fear—the comforting Holy Spirit is in you.*

the fear of the Lord, and in the **comfort** of the Holy Ghost, were multiplied.

Acts 9:31

I actually heard someone say that when he and his wife have an argument, he doesn't like it. But when they make up, he really likes that! He nearly enjoys having the fight. In a sense, that's the way it is when people come out against you or when you get attacked by the devil. I hope and pray you know that the comfort of the Holy Spirit is so good that you can nearly rejoice in tribulation.

> *That I may know him, and the power of his resurrection, and the fellowship of his sufferings, being made conformable unto his death.*

Philippians 3:10

The apostle Paul wanted to know Christ and the power of His resurrection, even His sufferings—knowing that the Holy Spirit supernaturally comforts. When people are ragging on you and bad things happen, never fear—the comforting Holy Spirit is in you.

10

Sin, Righteousness, Judgment

*And when he is come, he will reprove the world of **sin, and of righteousness, and of judgment**: of sin, because they believe not on me; of righteousness, because I go to my Father, and ye see me no more; of judgment, because the prince of this world is judged.*

John 16:8-11

I n John 16:7-11, the truth that Jesus shared with His disciples begins with all the benefits that the Holy Spirit brings with Him. Then He dives into the serious subjects of sin, righteousness, and judgment. The Holy Spirit will reprove and rebuke the world.

Most people think that "reproof" means God is going to nail you every time you do something wrong. Yet the scripture actually says He reproves people of the sin of not believing in Him. He wants all to come to the saving knowledge of salvation.

The Holy Spirit is not going to nail a person who doesn't know the Lord about what they're doing—all their sins; He's going to focus on the need for salvation.

> *The root of sin is not trusting the Lord.*

If you are born again and you sin, He deals with you about the root of sin—in other words, not trusting Jesus. The root of sin is not trusting the Lord, or leaning on yourself or others rather than leaning on Him. So He reproves you of not believing in Him.

And then the Holy Spirit reproves you of righteousness—not unrighteousness. Too many people interpret this verse that He will show you all your unrighteousness. No, it says He will convict you of *righteousness.* He will show you that you are the righteousness of God. Most people believe it's the opposite, which is one of the reasons they don't appreciate the ministry of the Holy Spirit. They attribute to Him all their guilt and condemnation. But He doesn't do that—you do. He shows you your righteousness.

> *He will show you that you are the righteousness of God.*

And then His Word says He will reprove you of judgment. And specifically, he says, because the prince of this world is judged. This isn't talking about you being judged. This is saying you're the winner. Satan is the one who's judged. Satan's the loser. He has been judged and there will be a final judgment.

Too many Christians think that the Holy Spirit's ministry is negative—that He comes to show your sin, unrighteousness, and to judge you. No. The Holy Spirit's ministry is positive—He is for you and empowers you to do God's will. He's your *Helper, Comforter, Advocate, Intercessor, Counselor, Strengthener, Standby*. Rejoice!

> *The Holy Spirit's ministry is positive— He is for you and empowers you to do God's will.*

Conclusion

The Positive Ministry of the Holy Spirit

Most people have been led to believe that self-doubt, self-condemnation, feelings of unworthiness, and conviction for individual sins are the work of the Holy Spirit. But that is *not* true!

I spend a great deal of time teaching on the unconditional love and grace of God. That is what changed my life. But I can tell by the questions and comments I get that many people still don't get it.

Because of that, years ago I asked the Lord to give me a way of expressing His grace that people can't miss. He gave me one of the most important revelations I ever had about the positive ministry of the Holy Spirit. Not everyone likes this, but they understand what I'm saying.

The devil's favorite tool is religion, and he has done a great job of convincing the body of Christ that the Holy Spirit is the source of negative feelings. He has convinced believers that the Holy Spirit shows and tells them that they are unworthy and have to "clean up their acts" if they ever want to receive from the Lord.

> *The Holy Spirit is never the source of any of your guilt or condemnation.*

The truth is, your heart—or more specifically your conscience—condemns you, not God. That is *not* the work of the Holy Spirit. The Holy Spirit is never the source of any of your guilt or condemnation. He does *not* make you feel bad when you sin. *Your conscience condemns you.* And when you are feeling unworthy, it's almost impossible to receive from God.

First John 3:19-21 says:

And hereby we know that we are of the truth, and shall assure our hearts before him. For if our heart condemn us, God is greater than our heart, and knoweth all things. Beloved, if our heart condemn us not, then have we confidence toward God.

This scripture passage makes it very clear that your heart can condemn you even though God is not. What a radical truth, which comes as a complete shock to most Christians.

We've just assumed that it is always the Holy Spirit who is condemning us.

If you can reach the point where your conscience is not condemning you, judging you, and causing you to feel unworthy to receive, then you will have confidence toward God, which has *"great recompence of reward"* (Heb. 10:35).

Most Christians never reach that place. Most know that God can answer their prayer; they just don't have the confidence that He will, because they feel unworthy. *They aren't willing to stand in faith, because feelings of guilt and unworthiness, which they mistakenly believe are coming from the Holy Spirit, shipwreck their faith.*

> *Holding faith, and a good conscience; which some having put away concerning faith have made shipwreck.*
> **1 Timothy 1:19**

Our conscience is not something we can or should ignore; it can be trained for our benefit, but it is *not* the Holy Spirit. The best way to deal with the conscience is to, as much as possible, not give it any occasion against us. It can't condemn you if you aren't giving it a reason.

Jesus calls the Holy Spirit the "Helper (Comforter)," not the afflicter.

However, no one lives a perfect life, and ultimately you have to purge your conscience from dead works.

- Hebrews 9:14 says, *"How much more shall the blood of Christ, who through the eternal Spirit offered himself without spot to God, purge your conscience from dead works to serve the living God?"*

- Hebrews 10:22 says, *"Let us draw near with a true heart in full assurance of faith, having our hearts sprinkled from an evil conscience."*

- And in Hebrews 4:16 we read, *"Let us therefore come boldly unto the throne of grace, that we may obtain mercy, and find grace to help in time of need."*

The ministry of the Holy Spirit is the opposite of what many Christians think. In John 14:16 we read how Jesus describes the Holy Spirit: *"And I will pray the Father, and he shall give you another Comforter, that he may abide with you for ever."*

Notice that *Jesus calls the Holy Spirit the "Helper (Comforter)," not the afflicter.* It also says that He will send "another" Comforter. "Another" means one of the same caliber, the same kind. Jesus was and still is a Comforter; He didn't condemn people during His earthly ministry.

*For **God sent not his Son into the world to condemn** the world; but that the world through him might be saved. He that believeth on him is not condemned: but* *he that believeth not is condemned already, because he hath not believed in the name of the only begotten Son of God. And this is the condemnation, that light is come into the world, and men loved darkness rather than light, because their deeds were evil.*

John 3:17-19

The Holy Spirit doesn't convict us of lying, stealing, adultery, murder, or the like—He convicts us that we aren't trusting in Jesus. That's the root of every sin. Technically, *people don't go to hell for their individual sins;* Jesus has already forgiven all of them (see 1 John 2:2). People go to hell for the single sin of not making Jesus their personal Savior, the complete and only payment for their sin. Even after receiving salvation, it's not our actions (sins) that are the problem but the heart attitude of not trusting Jesus.

The Holy Spirit should be your best Friend. He was sent here to encourage you and constantly assure you of God's love. He is the most important and most powerful person in your life. If

The Holy Spirit should be your best Friend.

you haven't been thinking correctly about the Holy Spirit, it's time to change your thinking. You will never be able to relate to God correctly until you understand this positive ministry of the Holy Spirit.

My new and expanded series, *The Positive Ministry of the Holy Spirit*, will help you make this change in your thinking. The Holy Spirit is the great Comforter, but His positive ministry goes far beyond that. If you want power in your life, you have to know and understand what I teach in this series.

Receive Jesus as Your Savior

Choosing to receive Jesus Christ as your Lord and Savior is the most important decision you'll ever make!

God's Word promises, *"That if thou shalt confess with thy mouth the Lord Jesus, and shalt believe in thine heart that God hath raised him from the dead, thou shalt be saved. For with the heart man believeth unto righteousness; and with the mouth confession is made unto salvation"* (Rom. 10:9–10). *"For whosoever shall call upon the name of the Lord shall be saved"* (Rom. 10:13).

By His grace, God has already done everything to provide salvation. Your part is simply to believe and receive. Pray out loud: "Jesus, I confess that You are my Lord and Savior. I believe in my heart that God raised You from the dead. By faith in Your Word, I receive salvation now. Thank You for saving me."

The very moment you commit your life to Jesus Christ, the truth of His Word instantly comes to pass in your spirit. Now that you're born again, there's a brand-new you!

Receive the Holy Spirit

As His child, your loving heavenly Father wants to give you the supernatural power you need to live a new life.

For every one that asketh receiveth; and he that seeketh findeth; and to him that knocketh it shall be opened... how much more shall your heavenly Father give the Holy Spirit to them that ask him?

Luke 11:10–13

All you have to do is ask, believe, and receive!

Pray: "Father, I recognize my need for Your power to live a new life. Please fill me with Your Holy Spirit. By faith, I receive it right now. Thank You for baptizing me. Holy Spirit, You are welcome in my life."

Congratulations! Now you're filled with God's supernatural power.

Some syllables from a language you don't recognize will rise up from your heart to your mouth (see 1 Cor. 14:14). As you speak them out loud by faith, you're releasing God's power from within and building yourself up in the spirit (see 1 Cor. 14:4). You can do this whenever and wherever you like.

It doesn't really matter whether you felt anything or not when you prayed to receive the Lord and His Spirit. If you believed in your heart that you received, then God's Word promises you did. *"Therefore I say unto you, What things soever ye desire, when ye pray, believe that ye receive them, and ye shall have them"* (Mark 11:24). God always honors His Word—believe it!

Please contact me and let me know that you've prayed to receive Jesus as your Savior or be filled with the Holy Spirit. I would like to rejoice with you and help you understand more fully what has taken place in your life. I'll send you a free gift that will help you understand and grow in your new relationship with the Lord.

Welcome to your new life!

Call for Prayer

I f you need prayer for any reason, you can call our Prayer Line 24 hours a day, seven days a week at 719-635-1111. A trained prayer minister will answer your call and pray with you. Every day, we receive testimonies of healings and other miracles from our Prayer Line, and we are ministering God's nearly-too-good-to-be-true message of the gospel to more people than ever. So I encourage you to call today!

About the Author

ANDREW WOMMACK'S life was forever changed the moment he encountered the supernatural love of God on March 23, 1968. As a renowned Bible teacher and author, Andrew has made it his mission to change the way the world sees God.

Andrew's vision is to go as far and deep with the gospel as possible. His message goes far through the *Gospel Truth* television program, which is available to nearly half the world's population. The message goes deep through discipleship at Charis Bible College, headquartered in Woodland Park, Colorado. Founded in 1994, Charis has campuses across the United States and around the globe.

Andrew also has an extensive library of teaching materials in print, audio, and video—most of which can be accessed for free from his website: awmi.net.

CONTACT INFORMATION

Andrew Wommack Ministries Inc.

PO Box 3333

Colorado Springs CO 80934-3333

Email: info@awmi.net

Helpline: 719-635-1111

Helpline available 24/7.

Website: www.awmi.net